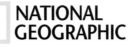

How Many?

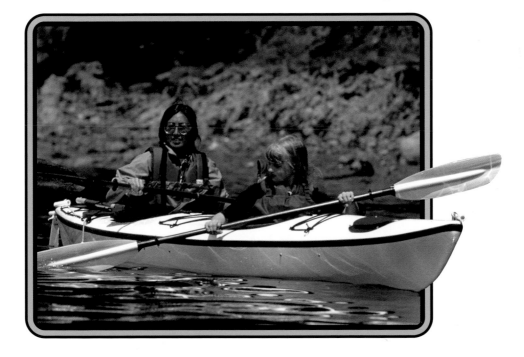

Rachel Elliott

How many people
are on the bicycle?

One person is on the bicycle.

How many people are in the boat?

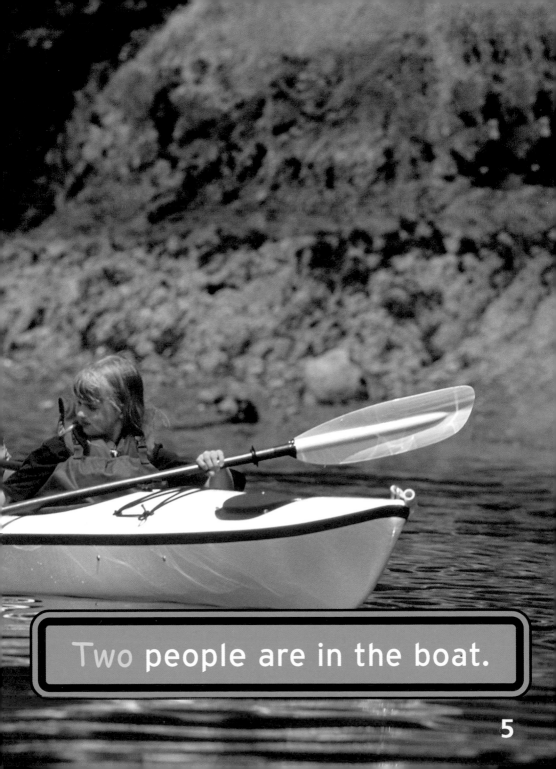

Two people are in the boat.

How many people are in the car?

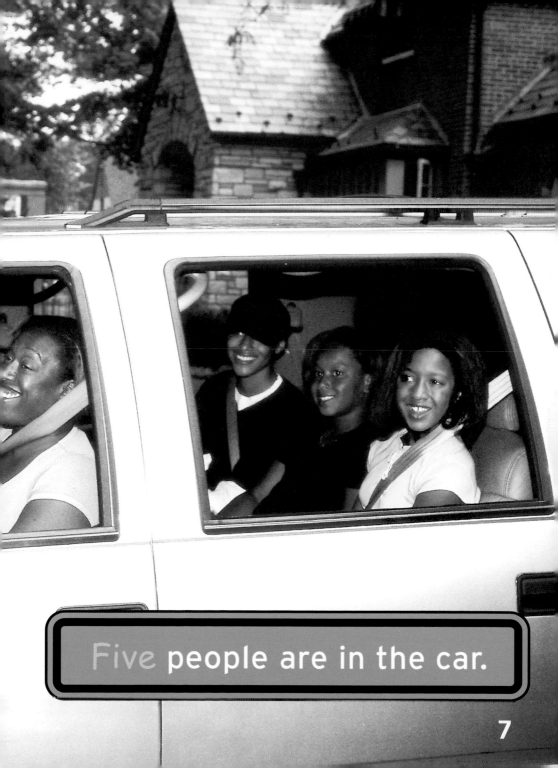

Five people are in the car.

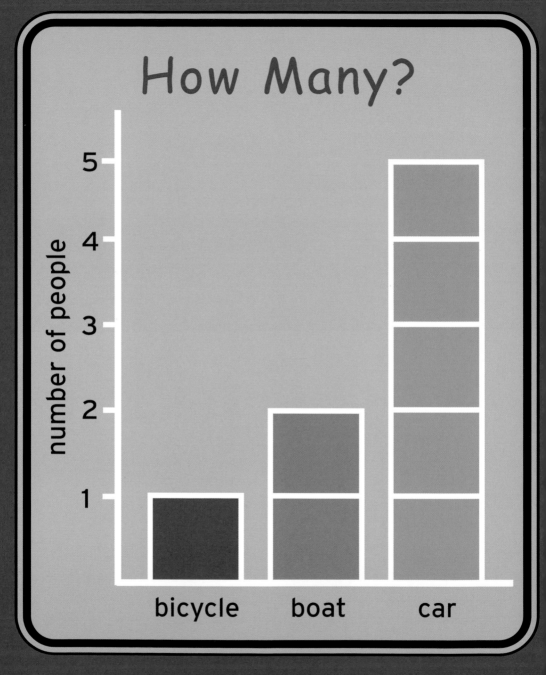

How Many?